8 Wastes Observation Form

DEFECTS

T0111900

OVERPRODUCTION

WAITING

TRANSPORTATION

INVENTORY

MOTION

EXTRA PROCESSING

NON-UTILIZED TALENTS

ENNA
KNOWLEDGE INTO PRACTICE

www.enna.com
www.productivitypress.com

8 Wastes Observation Form

DEFECTS

OVERPRODUCTION

WAITING

TRANSPORTATION

INVENTORY

MOTION

EXTRA PROCESSING

NON-UTILIZED TALENTS

8 Wastes Observation Form

DEFECTS

OVERPRODUCTION

WAITING

TRANSPORTATION

INVENTORY

MOTION

EXTRA PROCESSING

NON-UTILIZED TALENTS

8 Wastes Observation Form

DEFECTS

OVERPRODUCTION

WAITING

TRANSPORTATION

INVENTORY

MOTION

EXTRA PROCESSING

NON-UTILIZED TALENTS

8 Wastes Observation Form

DEFECTS

OVERPRODUCTION

WAITING

TRANSPORTATION

INVENTORY

MOTION

EXTRA PROCESSING

NON-UTILIZED TALENTS

ENNA
KNOWLEDGE INTO PRACTICE

A **Productivity Press** Product

www.enna.com
www.productivitypress.com

8 Wastes Observation Form

DEFECTS

OVERPRODUCTION

WAITING

TRANSPORTATION

INVENTORY

MOTION

EXTRA PROCESSING

NON-UTILIZED TALENTS

ENNA
KNOWLEDGE INTO PRACTICE

A **Productivity Press** Product

www.enna.com
www.productivitypress.com

8 Wastes Observation Form

DEFECTS

OVERPRODUCTION

WAITING

TRANSPORTATION

INVENTORY

MOTION

EXTRA PROCESSING

NON-UTILIZED TALENTS

8 Wastes Observation Form

DEFECTS

OVERPRODUCTION

WAITING

TRANSPORTATION

INVENTORY

MOTION

EXTRA PROCESSING

NON-UTILIZED TALENTS

ENNA
KNOWLEDGE INTO PRACTICE

A **Productivity Press** Product

www.enna.com
www.productivitypress.com

8 Wastes Observation Form

DEFECTS

OVERPRODUCTION

WAITING

TRANSPORTATION

INVENTORY

MOTION

EXTRA PROCESSING

NON-UTILIZED TALENTS

8 Wastes Observation Form

DEFECTS

OVERPRODUCTION

WAITING

TRANSPORTATION

INVENTORY

MOTION

EXTRA PROCESSING

NON-UTILIZED TALENTS

ENNA
KNOWLEDGE INTO PRACTICE

www.enna.com
www.productivitypress.com

8 Wastes Observation Form

DEFECTS

OVERPRODUCTION

WAITING

TRANSPORTATION

INVENTORY

MOTION

EXTRA PROCESSING

NON-UTILIZED TALENTS

8 Wastes Observation Form

DEFECTS

OVERPRODUCTION

WAITING

TRANSPORTATION

INVENTORY

MOTION

EXTRA PROCESSING

NON-UTILIZED TALENTS

KNOWLEDGE INTO PRACTICE

A **Productivity Press** Product

www.enna.com
www.productivitypress.com

8 Wastes Observation Form

DEFECTS

OVERPRODUCTION

WAITING

TRANSPORTATION

INVENTORY

MOTION

EXTRA PROCESSING

NON-UTILIZED TALENTS

ENNA
KNOWLEDGE INTO PRACTICE

A **Productivity Press** Product

www.enna.com
www.productivitypress.com

8 Wastes Observation Form

DEFECTS

OVERPRODUCTION

WAITING

TRANSPORTATION

INVENTORY

MOTION

EXTRA PROCESSING

NON-UTILIZED TALENTS

ENNA
KNOWLEDGE INTO PRACTICE

A **Productivity Press** Product

www.enna.com
www.productivitypress.com

8 Wastes Observation Form

DEFECTS

OVERPRODUCTION

WAITING

TRANSPORTATION

INVENTORY

MOTION

EXTRA PROCESSING

NON-UTILIZED TALENTS

ENNA
KNOWLEDGE INTO PRACTICE

A **Productivity Press** Product

www.enna.com
www.productivitypress.com

8 Wastes Observation Form

DEFECTS

OVERPRODUCTION

WAITING

TRANSPORTATION

INVENTORY

MOTION

EXTRA PROCESSING

NON-UTILIZED TALENTS

ENNA
KNOWLEDGE INTO PRACTICE

A **Productivity Press** Product

www.enna.com
www.productivitypress.com

8 Wastes Observation Form

DEFECTS

OVERPRODUCTION

WAITING

TRANSPORTATION

INVENTORY

MOTION

EXTRA PROCESSING

NON-UTILIZED TALENTS

8 Wastes Observation Form

DEFECTS

OVERPRODUCTION

WAITING

TRANSPORTATION

INVENTORY

MOTION

EXTRA PROCESSING

NON-UTILIZED TALENTS

8 Wastes Observation Form

ENNA
KNOWLEDGE INTO PRACTICE

A **Productivity Press** Product

www.enna.com
www.productivitypress.com

8 Wastes Observation Form

DEFECTS

OVERPRODUCTION

WAITING

TRANSPORTATION

INVENTORY

MOTION

EXTRA PROCESSING

NON-UTILIZED TALENTS

8 Wastes Observation Form

DEFECTS

OVERPRODUCTION

WAITING

TRANSPORTATION

INVENTORY

MOTION

EXTRA PROCESSING

NON-UTILIZED TALENTS

ENNA
KNOWLEDGE INTO PRACTICE

A **Productivity Press** Product

www.enna.com
www.productivitypress.com

8 Wastes Observation Form

DEFECTS

OVERPRODUCTION

WAITING

TRANSPORTATION

INVENTORY

MOTION

EXTRA PROCESSING

NON-UTILIZED TALENTS

ENNA
KNOWLEDGE INTO PRACTICE

A **Productivity Press** Product

www.enna.com
www.productivitypress.com

8 Wastes Observation Form

DEFECTS

OVERPRODUCTION

WAITING

TRANSPORTATION

INVENTORY

MOTION

EXTRA PROCESSING

NON-UTILIZED TALENTS

ENNA
KNOWLEDGE INTO PRACTICE

www.enna.com
www.productivitypress.com

8 Wastes Observation Form

DEFECTS

OVERPRODUCTION

WAITING

TRANSPORTATION

INVENTORY

MOTION

EXTRA PROCESSING

NON-UTILIZED TALENTS

ENNA
KNOWLEDGE INTO PRACTICE

A **Productivity Press** Product

8 Wastes Observation Form

DEFECTS

OVERPRODUCTION

WAITING

TRANSPORTATION

INVENTORY

MOTION

EXTRA PROCESSING

NON-UTILIZED TALENTS

ENNA
KNOWLEDGE INTO PRACTICE

A **Productivity Press** Product

www.enna.com
www.productivitypress.com